VALENTINE'S DAY JOKES

FOR KIDS

MAYAN HARRIS

Knock Knock!
Who's there?
Juno!
Juno who?
Juno I love you,
right?

What did the boy sheep say to the girl sheep on Valentine's Day?

"I love ewe."

What did the girl sheep say to the boy sheep on Valentine's Day?

"Hey, you're not so baaaa-d yourself!"

Did you hear what happened after Mr. Goodbar and Peppermint Patty got married?

They had a baby, Ruth.

What is an alien's
favorite chocolate?

A Mars bar!

What happened when two vampires went on a blind date?

It was love at first bite!

What happened to
the price of flowers
on Valentine's Day?

They rose to the
occasion.

A boy finds a frog that says, "Kiss me and I will become a beautiful princess." The boy looks at the frog and puts it in his pocket. "Hey," the frog says, "don't you want me to turn into a princess?" "Nah," the boy says, "I'd rather have a talking frog."

What did Batman
give Catwoman on
Valentine's Day?

A mouse.

Why couldn't the skeleton dance at the Valentine's Day party?

Because he had no body to dance with!

What kind of chocolate do they sell at the airport?

Plane Chocolate!

Knock Knock!
Who's There?
Kenya!
Kenya who?
"Kenya feel the love
tonight?"

What did one flame say to the other on Valentine's Day?

"We're a perfect match."

Why did the man send his wife's Valentine through Twitter?

Because she is his tweetheart.

Why are veins so sensitive about blood?

They take it to heart.

What did one calculator say to the other on Valentine's Day?

"How do I love thee? Let me count the ways."

Man: I really love hotels.

Woman: If you love them so much, why don't you Marriott?!

What does a chocolate bar do when it hears a good joke?

It Snickers.

What happens when
you fall in love with
a French chef?

You get buttered up.

What happened to the oyster at the Valentine's Day dance?

It pulled a mussel!

Did you hear about the man who promised his girlfriend a diamond for Valentine's Day?

He took her to a baseball game.

What was the French cat's favorite Valentine's Day dessert?

Chocolate mousse

What do you call
two birds in love?

Tweethearts.

What did the light
bulb say to his wife?

"I love you watts
and watts!"

Why did the boy put a candy bar under his pillow?

So he would have sweet dreams!

Why did the girl put clothes on the Valentine's Day card she was sending?

She thought it needed to be ad-dressed.

What do you call a sheep covered in chocolate?

A Hershey baaaaa.

What is the most romantic city in England?

Loverpool.

What did the ghost
call his sweetheart?

His goul-friend.

Knock, knock.
Who's There?
Alec.
Alec Who?
Alec to kiss you on
the cheek!

What did one piece of string say to the other on February 14th?

"Be my valen-twine."

What did the valentine say to the stamp?

"Stick with me, and we'll go places!"

What did the M&M
go to college?

Because he wanted
to be a Smarty.

Knock Knock!
Who's there?
Frank.
Frank Who?
Frank you for being
my Valentine.

Where do fortune tellers dance on Valentine's Day?

At the crystal ball.

What did the
farmer give his wife
for Valentine's Day?

Hogs and kisses.

Did you hear about the snake love letter?

He sealed it with a hiss.

What did the circle
say to the triangle
on Valentine's Day?

I think you're acute.

What does a carpet salesman give his wife for Valentine's Day?

Rugs and kisses.

What did the boy octopus say to the girl octopus?

"I wanna hold your hand, hand, hand, hand, hand, hand, hand, hand."

What did cavemen give their wives on Valentine's Day?

Lots of "ughs" and kisses.

What did the blueberry say to his wife on Valentine's Day?

"I love you berry much."

What did the man call his wife who gave him a wallet made of soft leather?

His suede heart.

What do you get when you cross a dog with a valentine card?

A card that says "I love you, drool-ly. Drool-ly, I do!"

What did the lamp
say to the switch?

"You turn me on."

What did one muffin say to the other on Valentine' Day?

You're my stud muffin!

What is a ram's favorite saying on February 14th?

I only have eyes for ewe, deer.

Why do skunks celebrate Valentine's Day?

Because they're scent-imental.

What did the girl cat say to the boy cat on Valentine's Day?

"You're purrr-fect for me."

Why do magicians love chocolate?

Because they perform a lot of Twix.

What happened
when the two tennis
players met?

It was lob at first
sight.

Made in the USA
Lexington, KY
07 February 2019